Patient Name: **Your** Date:
Address:

R_X

for

Fear

Word of God
Jesus

MD:
Signature:

Removing the fear factors
in your life. Live Restored
through the Word of God.

Perfect Love > Fear

Michelle Bollom

Introduction

The Promises in the Bible are God Breathed.
2 Timothy 3:16 MSG
Every part of Scripture is God-breathed and useful one way or another—showing us truth, exposing our rebellion, correcting our mistakes, training us to live God's way. Through the Word we are put together and shaped up for the tasks God has for us.

The Word is what started it all. **The Word was God from day one.** John 1:1-5 MSG
The Word was first, the Word present to God, God present to the Word. The Word was God, in readiness for God from day one. Everything was created through him; nothing—not one thing! -came into being without him. What came into existence was Life, and the Life was Light to live by. The Life-Light blazed out of the darkness; the darkness couldn't put it out.

The Word became flesh and dwells among us.
John 1:14 ESV
And the Word became flesh and dwelt among us, and we have seen His glory, glory as of the only Son from the Father, full of grace and truth.

God is Love. 1 John 4:8
God is love. (Perfect Love)

No fear in love. Perfect Love drives out fear.
1 John 4:18 CEB
There is no fear in love. But perfect love drives out fear.

If these Bible verses are not enough to convince you that there is tremendous power in the Word of God, I hope to convince you as you take a journey with me for the next month on what I call Your Rx for Fear.

Fear is Faith in the wrong god. Fear is the most socially accepted sin in the Church. Fear is a serial killer, the prime suspect in the death of more people on the planet than all other diseases combined. Fear in every form has been linked to heart disease, cancer, autoimmune disorders, mental illness and many other sicknesses. Fear is the welcome mat to demonic activity in our lives. Fear is quietly stealing our destiny, killing our bodies and destroying our cities. Fear clouds our convictions and distorts our discernment.
~ Kris Vallotton

I, like so many people, have battled with fear. For years, I stayed trapped in fear, dread, worry and anxiety. Fear keeps us paralyzed and never moving into the plans and purposes God has for us. Just like the quote above says; Fear is linked to all sorts of illness and sickness.

When I first started reading the Word I would search various scripture by topics and then search various translations and turn them into first person prayers. I used to call them *Prayer Scripts* and would make them for people for various issues they were facing. I did it for myself as I walked through the breaking of an addiction to nicotine. I had tried countless methods for years, but the Power of the Holy Spirit and the Promises in God's Word are what ultimately and finally delivered me.

My hope and prayer for you is that you will fall in love with the abundant Promises available to you in God's word. After all, it is His ultimate Love Letter to us, and you will begin to experience the power of His Word for yourself. Get ready to step out of fear and move into the abundant life God has for you.

This book is going to help remove the Fear Factors and replace them with Faith Factors as you declare and decree each day God's amazing promises on fear out loud and say the accompanying prayer. You will see as you keep doing it each day that you too will let go and be cured of the fear that has been making you sick, stealing your destiny, and clouding your convictions and distorting your discernment.

Come take this journey to kick that nasty fear to the curb for good.

Where there was fear, Lord, You bring courage!

<u>One</u>

God is love. There is no fear in love: dread does not exist. But perfect complete, full-grown Love drives out fear. ~1 John 4:8,18 AMP

Lord I seem to only know what imperfect love looks like. I sometimes cannot even grasp the kind of love You are offering me. My love is so often childish and conditional. Your perfect, unconditional, and complete love is what I want. Perfect Love, found in You and You alone is what I seek. Remind me always when fear tries to hijack my day that You, God, Perfect Love, is what drives out fear and keeps it away. Only Your love promises to drive out every bit of fear, anxiety, dread and worry from my life.

Two

I am strong and courageous, and take action; I do not fear nor am I dismayed, for the Lord God, my God, is with me. He will not fail me nor abandon me. He will guide me.
~1 Chronicles 28:20 AMP

Lord, help me to take action and no longer be paralyzed in fear. Even if I must do it afraid, help me to do it. Thank You that Your promise is that You will not fail or abandon me. Guide me Lord with each shaky, unsteady step until I can confidently and courageously walk in the plans and purposes You have for me.

<u>Three</u>

When I march out to battle and see a fighting force larger than mine, I won't be afraid of them, because the Lord my God, the one who brought me up from Egypt, is with me. As I advance toward the war, I am not discouraged! I am not afraid! I do not panic! I will not shake in fear on account of them, because the Lord my God is going with me to fight my enemies for me and to save me.

~Deuteronomy 20:1-4 CEB

Lord, when oppositions and attacks come my way and it appears so much larger than me and what I can handle or bear, remind me that You are faithful and always with me.

I do not need to panic because I know You have done it before and that You promise to fight my battles and save me from all harm. I simply trust You to guide me when to advance or when to stand firm. You are the one going with me to work and wage war on my behalf.

Four

I shall not be in dread or fear of anything for the Lord my God is in my midst, a great and awesome God.

~Deuteronomy 7:21 ESV

Dread is never from You, Lord. Help me to recognize the enemy's attempt to bring dread into my thoughts. I take my thoughts captive to the obedience of Your Word. Dread and fear are unable to exist in Your midst. Renew my mind Lord. You are a great and awesome God. I am anticipating great and mighty things and am anxious for nothing.

Five

I am strong and brave, and I will not
tremble in fear of them, because the
Eternal my God is going with me.
He'll never fail me or abandon me!
~Deuteronomy 31:6 VOICE

Today and every day I am not alone.
Thank You, God, for always going with me.
I will not tremble. I am strong and brave
because of You and Your Spirit working
within me. When people fail or abandon
me, thank You God that You never do.

<u>Six</u>

So that I may boldly say, The Lord is my helper, and I will not fear what man shall do unto me. ~Hebrews 13:6 JUB

Lord, some days I feel that it is me against the world, but that is just not true. I always have a helper in You. I can boldly exclaim this Promise and know that no one can do anything to me that You will not work out for my ultimate good.

<u>Seven</u>

God is my salvation, I trust, and fear not, for my strength and song is Jehovah, and He is to me for salvation.
~Isaiah 12:2 YLT

Thank you Lord that You are my salvation. I trust in You. Thank you for being my strength and my song when I feel weary and my praise may have grown dim. Stir up my praise and help me to sing loudly today to drive away all fearful thoughts.

<u>Eight</u>

Strengthen my feeble hands, steady my knees that give way; I say to my fearful heart, be strong, do not fear; my God will come, He will come with vengeance; with divine retribution, He will come to save me. ~Isaiah 35:3-4 NIV

Lord, help me to remain steady and strong knowing that when I simply wait on You; You come - with a vengeance to save me.

<u>Nine</u>

I fear not, for God is with me; I am not dismayed, for my God; will strengthen me, He will help me, He will uphold me with His righteous right hand.

~Isaiah 41:10 ESV

When the news or people try to dismay me Lord, remind me that I am not dismayed because You strengthen and uphold me with Your righteous right hand. I fear not because you are with me. I will not be dismayed because I know You will help me.

<u>Ten</u>

The Lord my God, who grasps my strong hand, says to me, don't fear; I will help you.
~ Isaiah 43:13 CEB

Oh, Lord, some days I feel like I am slipping and drowning in discouragement and fear. Help me to remove the distracting negative voices around me and remember that You grasp me by my hand and help me out of any situation. May I simply raise my hands in praise and perfect surrender unto You. Rescue me Lord.

<u>Eleven</u>

But now thus says the Lord, He who created me, who formed me: "Fear not, for I have redeemed you; I have called you by name, you are mine. When you pass through the waters,
I will be with you; and through the rivers, they shall not overwhelm you; when you walk through fire you shall not be burned, and the flame shall not consume you. For I am the Lord your God, the Holy One of Israel, your Savior. ~Isaiah 43:1-3 ESV

Oh, Lord, how awesome a Savior You are! Thank you that when I feel like I am going to drown or go up in flames, You promise that I will not be overcome. You have redeemed me and called me by name. I am so grateful that You do not let the flames of trials or disappointments consume me.

<u>Twelve</u>

Peace God leaves with me; His perfect peace He gives to me; not as the world gives does He give to me. I do not let my heart be troubled, nor let it be afraid. I let God's perfect peace calm me in every circumstance and give me courage and strength for every challenge. ~John 14:27 AMP

Lord, there are so many things the world will try to convince me brings peace, but in truth they don't bring lasting peace at all. Thank You for Perfect Peace for every circumstance that I will face. Thank You Lord for the courage and strength You provide for every challenge.

<u>Thirteen</u>

In this world, I will be plagued with times of trouble, but I need not fear; For Jesus, has triumphed over this corrupt world order.
~John 16:33 VOICE

Thank You Lord that You triumphed over this corrupt world. With You I will triumph over every trial, temptation and trouble that I encounter too.

Fourteen

I am strong and courageous. I am not afraid; I am not discouraged, for the Lord my God will be with me wherever I go.

~Joshua 1:9 NIV

Lord, some days it seems like I am fearful or dreadful what the day will hold and can become so discouraged before my feet even hit the ground. Thank You that You remind me that I am strong and courageous. I need not ever be afraid or discouraged, because You are with me at all times regardless of where I have to go.

<u>Fifteen</u>

I am God's Beloved. I am worth so much more than a whole flock of sparrows. God knows everything about me, even the number of hairs on my head. So, I do not fear. ~Matthew 10:30-31 VOICE

What a beautiful promise that I am Your Beloved, and You Lord say to me that I am worth so much to you. You know everything about me. You know every failing or flourishing. Every single hair on my head is not beyond Your knowledge. Thank You that when I don't know what or where or how, You know it all. I have no reason to fear.

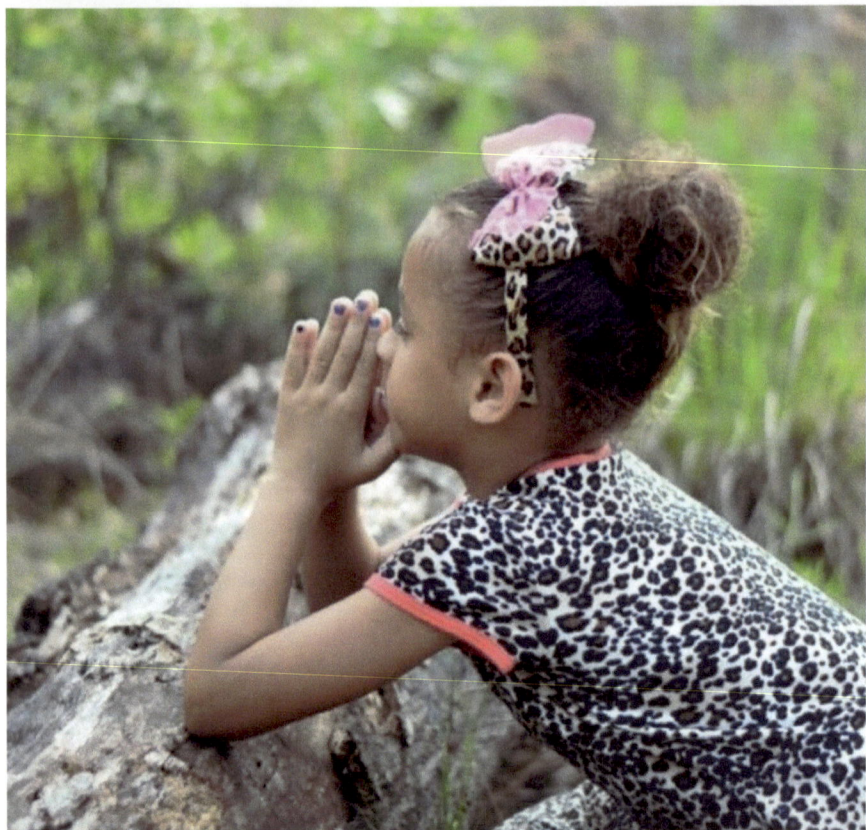

Sixteen

Be still. *Jesus is with me.* **I have nothing to fear.** ~Matthew 14:27 VOICE

Lord, calm my mind and help me to sit still and not force or rush things in my own strength. Help me to get quiet before You so that I can sense Your mighty presence within me.

<u>Seventeen</u>

I will rise and have no fear.
~Matthew 17:7 ESV

Thank You Lord for a new day with new mercies. Thank You that I can rise each day without fear because You promise that in Jesus, I have no reason to fear and am made strong where I feel weak.

Eighteen

The fear of human opinion disables; trusting in God protects me from that.
~Proverbs 29:25 MSG

Lord, opinions are always swirling around me. Sometimes others opinions are forced on me and sometimes I can try to force my opinion on others. Forgive me when I hold the belief that human opinion is more important than what You are asking of me. Lord help me to not be disabled by fear of man and human opinion. Thank You Lord that You promise if I follow after You, You will protect me from that.

<u>Nineteen</u>

In God, I will praise His word, in God I have put my trust; I will not fear what flesh can do unto me. ~ Psalm 56:4 JUB

Thank You Lord for all Your promises. Thank You for Your Word that is powerful. Thank You for salvation and Your Son, Jesus, whom I have placed my trust in. Because of Jesus, and His resurrection power living inside me, I have no reason to ever fear what mere flesh tries to do to me.

<u>Twenty</u>

I will not fear though tens of thousands assail me on every side. ~Psalm 3:6 NIV

Lord, some days it feels like everyone is against me. I feel the attacks on every side and it can seem like tens of thousands. What a glorious promise that with God, I am always a majority over all those tens of thousands that try to assail me. Thank You Lord for Your protection.

<u>Twenty-One</u>

Even in the unending shadows of death's darkness, I am not overcome by fear. Because You are with me in those dark moments, near with Your protection and guidance, I am comforted.
~Psalm 23:4 VOICE

Lord, I sometimes get bombarded with so much news of death and darkness. I thank You that in the dark moments You are near with Your protection and guidance to comfort me. Help me to pour out that comfort onto others to encourage them with the Light and Love of You.

Twenty-Two

The Lord is my light and my salvation— Whom shall I fear? The Lord is the refuge and fortress of my life— Whom shall I dread?

~Psalm 27:1 AMP

Lord, help me to always recognize that You are my light and my salvation. You alone are my refuge and fortress. I have no reason to fear or dread. Help me to be so plugged into You and Your power that my light will shine brightly to help others find You and Your refuge too.

<u>Twenty-Three</u>

God met me more than halfway, He freed me from my anxious fears.
~Psalm 34:4 MSG

Lord, I can go from zero to full on freak out some days. Thank You that You meet me more than halfway-You meet me all the way. Keep me focused on You and not the issues unfolding around me. Thank you that You alone free me from all my anxious fears.

<u>Twenty-Four</u>

God is my refuge and strength, a very present help in tribulation. Therefore, I will not fear. ~Psalm 46:1-2 JUB

Trials and tribulations can come upon me in an instant and I sometimes find myself turning to various things to bring me refuge and comfort that are not You. Lord, help me to recognize when I turn to something other than You to bring me refuge, comfort or strength and know that my very present help for all tribulation is only in You.

Twenty-Five

**When anxiety was great within me,
Your consolation brought me joy.**
~Psalm 94:19 NIV

**Anxiety can be so overwhelming
that I become deflated, downcast
and depressed. Help me to look to
You for consolation that will bring
me great joy.**

Twenty-Six

The Lord is on my side; I will not fear: what can man do unto me?
~Psalm 118:6 BRG

Lies, judgment, rejection, nasty jabs and curses can sometimes be flung all around me. Lord, help me not to retaliate and throw them back. Help me to recognize that whoever is against me does not matter because You are always on my side.

Twenty-Seven

In the face of
suffering,
I do not fear.

~Revelation 2:10 VOICE

Lord, each day I have a choice.
When I face suffering I can choose
to wallow or I can choose to worship.
Help me to worship even if through
gritted teeth so I can face any
suffering without fear because
You are with me.

Twenty-Eight

And I am convinced that nothing can ever separate me from God's love. Neither death nor life, neither angels nor demons, neither my fears for today nor my worries about tomorrow—not even the powers of hell can separate me from God's love. No power in the sky above or in the earth below—indeed, nothing in all creation will ever be able to separate me from the love of God that is revealed in Christ Jesus our Lord.
~Romans 8:38-39 NLT

Lord, help me to recognize that with You, Nothing, means Nothing. That I can be firmly convinced and unwavering in knowing that no powers, worries or fears, high or low can ever separate me from You or Your love.

Twenty-Nine

For God, has not given me a spirit of fear, but of power and of love and of a sound mind. ~2 Timothy 1:7 NKJV

When I am feeling powerless Lord, You give me power. When I am feeling unlovely, Lord You give me love. When my mind is bouncing off of every fear, swirling in doubt, You give me a sound mind.

<u>Thirty</u>

**God's Spirit remains in my midst...
So, I fear not!** ~Haggai 2:5 ESV

**When I operate in my flesh I can
crowd out and forget that Your
Spirit is within me. Lord, help me to
know that Your Spirit remains
always in my midst and I alone have
the choice to decide to walk in my
flesh or walk in Your Spirit to
remove fear.**

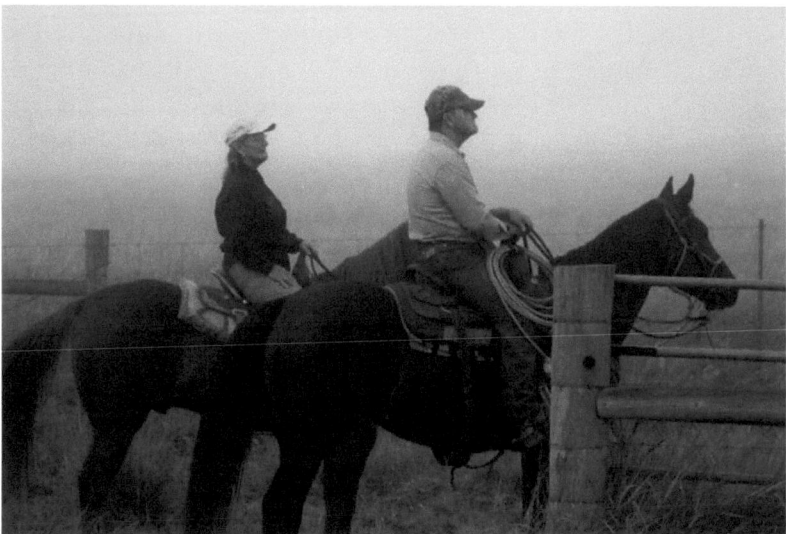

Thirty-One

He who dwells in the shelter of the Most High will remain secure and rest in the shadow of the Almighty whose power no enemy can withstand. I will say of the Lord, He is my refuge and my fortress, My God, in whom I trust with great confidence, and on whom I rely! For He will save me from the trap of the fowler, and from the deadly pestilence. He will cover me and completely protect me with His pinions, and under His wings I will find refuge; His faithfulness is a shield and a wall. I will not be afraid of the terror of night, nor of the arrow that flies by day, nor of the pestilence that stalks in darkness, nor of the destruction (sudden death) that lays waste at noon. A thousand may fall at my side and ten thousand at my right hand, but danger will not come near me. I will only be a spectator as I look on with my eyes and witness the divine repayment of the wicked as I watch safely from the shelter of the Most High. Because I have made the Lord, who is my refuge, even the Most High, my dwelling place, no evil will befall me, nor will any plague come near my tent. For He will command His angels regarding me, to protect and defend and guard me in all my ways of obedience and service. They will lift me up in their hands, so that I do not even strike my foot against a stone. I will tread upon the lion and cobra; The young lion and the serpent I will trample underfoot. Because I set my love on Him, therefore God will save me; He will set me securely on high, because I know His name and confidently trust and rely on Him, knowing God will never abandon me; no, never. I will call upon God and He will answer me; He will be with me in trouble; He will rescue me and honor me. With a long life God will satisfy me and God will let me see His salvation. ~Psalm 91:1-16 AMP

Lord, help me to dwell and abide with You always. Help me to take each of these words and decree and declare them over and over until they are firmly rooted within me to know that, without any doubt, You will never abandon me, no never. When I cry out to You, You always answer me. You will rescue me and honor me and give me the refuge and rest that can only be given by You. Your faithfulness is a shield to me. Your Perfect Love removes all Fear. Thank You Lord for the Promises in Your word and the Power of Your Holy Spirit within me. Let me remember to use these promises to step out of fear and to step into the courageous confidence You have called me to.

Photo Credits

1 Nature Reminds us "It's About Love"- Michelle Bollom
2 Under the Pier- Brittany Billings
3 Cattle Crossing- Ashleigh Rodriguez Photography
4 Antelope Canyon- Page, AZ- Iris Stephens
5 A Lone Sail Boat in the Gulf of Mexico- Kim Weingart
6 Breathtaking View of Bolu, Turkey- Gülsün Gülduran
7 The Empty Cross in Kerrville, TX- Joe Bollom
8 Rays of Hope- Iris Stephens
9 Petit Jean State Park- Morrilton, AR- Michelle Bollom
10 One Last Time- Rick Haasl
11 Waterfall in the Red Rocks of Sedona, AZ- Kim Weingart
12 Garden of Gethsemane, Jerusalem- Iris Stephens
13 Arial of New York City- Myranda Piña
14 Crack of Dawn- Calico, AR- Shay Arnold- West Photography
15 Eggs in a Robin's Nest- Joe Bollom
16 A Child's Prayer- Frank Gable
17 Sunrise in Fulton Harbor, TX- Michelle Bollom
18 Cotton Candy Clouds of TX- Myranda Piña
19 A Well Worn Bible- Frank Gable
20 Mount of Beatitudes in Israel- Michelle Bollom
21 Winter Trees Reaching for the Sky in Texas- Curran Bollom
22 Dove in Cleft of a Rock- Western Wall, Jerusalem- Iris Stephens
23 Restoration Line- Israel- Michelle Bollom
24 Mammoth Caves National Park, KY- Kim Weingart
25 Silver Lining- Tomball, TX- Michelle Bollom
26 Sun Dial in Savannah, GA- Michelle Bollom
27 Exiting the Cave- Petit Jean State Park, Morrilton, AR- Michelle Bollom
28 The Grand Canyon, AZ- Kim Weingart
29 Tulips in London- Romina Limbo
30 Through the Fog- Kristi McElroy
31 Wailing Wall Prayers- Jerusalem- Michelle Bollom

Continue to pray the Word
with these books in the
Prayer Scripts Series

Your Rx for Healing
Your Rx for Overcoming Temptation
Your Rx for Forgiveness
Your Rx for Peace
Your Rx for Joy
Your Rx for Hope
Your Rx for Purity

For further encouragement, please visit
www.restoredministries.org
restoredministriesblog.wordpress.com
Facebook-Twitter-Instagram-You Tube

#LiveRestored
#MindBodySoul